D1520250

The Chibcha Indians believed the Chibcha god, Chibchacum, supported the world on his shoulders. Whenever there was an earthquake they believed it was Chibchacum shifting his heavy burden.

www.rourkepublishing.com

Editor: Frank Sloan

Why Chibchacum carries the world is based on a Chibcha myth from Columbia and is retold by Sandy Sepehri.

Author's note: Numerous sources can be found on the internet and in encyclopedias on the 3 central characters in this story (Bochica, Chibchacum, and Chie.)

Illustrated by Brian Demeter
Cover design and storyboards by Nicola Stratford

To Shahri, with love
          S.S.

Library of Congress Cataloging-in-Publication Data

Sepehri, Sandy.
  Why Chibchacum carries the world : based on a Colombian myth / retold by Sandy Sepehri ; illustrated by Brian Demeter.
     p. cm. -- (Latin American tales and myths)
  ISBN 1-60044-215-3
 1. Chibcha mythology. 2. Chibcha Indians--Folklore. 3. Legends--Colombia. I. Demeter, Brian, ill. II. Title. III. Series.

   F2270.2.C4.S47 2007
   398.208998'2--dc22

                              2006014660

Printed in the USA

Latin American Tales and Myths

WHY CHIBCHACUM CARRIES THE WORLD

Based On A Chibcha Myth

Retold by Sandy Sepehri
Illustrated by Brian Demeter
Cover design and storyboards by Nicola Stratford
Project Consultant: Silvina Peralta Ramos

Rourke
Publishing LLC
Vero Beach, Florida 32964

Thousands of years ago, the South American country of **Colombia** was inhabited solely by Indian tribes. One of these tribes, the **Chibcha**, believed their world was ruled by two gods: **Bochica** and **Chibchacum**.

Bochica was kind and had ultimate power. He had created the world and its people. He even took the form of a man who walked through the land and taught his people how to behave and how to grow crops.

It is said that when he finished his teachings and left the Earth, his final footprint was saved on the surface of a western rock.

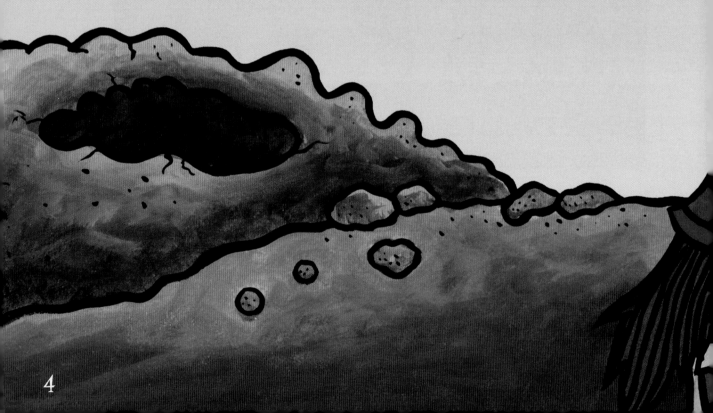

To the extent that Bochica was kind and loving, Chibchacum was cruel and mischievous. His cruelty and anger came from fear. He was afraid that the Chibcha people did not value him because he did not have Bochica's powers.

"Why did you bother to create me, Master?" Chibchacum scornfully asked Bochica one day.

"Because the love of which I am made is so great," answered Bochica, "that it grew and grew until pieces of it broke off. The first piece is you, Chibchacum, and the other pieces are the people. You are special and I have entrusted you with the important job of helping the people remember that they are all a part of me too, and that, one day, when they are ready, they will come back to me."

"Liar!" snapped Chibchacum. "I am useless! Why should you be the creator and I the created? You have all the power and I have nothing!

"I want to be the master of my own creations, not the guardian of yours!" shouted Chibchacum. "If I cannot have power, I will take yours."

Then, with the power of thought, Chibchacum transported himself to Earth to find ways to turn the people away from Bochica.

isguised as a man, he came to a village, where he met a beautiful woman named **Chie**. She thought Chibchacum was intensely handsome, and he promised to make her his queen in a world they could both dominate.

"We need to convince the people to worship me," Chibchacum said.

"But they worship Bochica," Chie responded.

"They do not have to worship me by name," Chibchacum said. "They need only reject the teachings of Bochica."

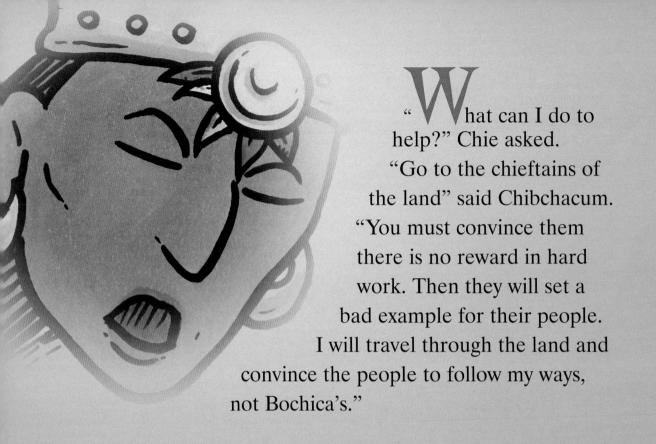

" What can I do to help?" Chie asked.

"Go to the chieftains of the land" said Chibchacum. "You must convince them there is no reward in hard work. Then they will set a bad example for their people. I will travel through the land and convince the people to follow my ways, not Bochica's."

All of this was music to the power-hungry Chie's ears. She set out to follow Chibchacum's orders and encouraged the people to seek temporary pleasures.

Meanwhile, Chibchacum traveled from the coast to the low-lying fields, spreading his dark philosophy like a contagious disease.

He entered the minds of the humble farmers and basket weavers, telling them to care more about their things than each other. He whispered lies in people's ears and turned them against one another. Worst of all, he spread the idea that certain groups are superior to others, thereby causing **bigotry** and provoking war.

"Look, my darling Chie," said Chibchacum one day. "Look at the people. They are truly mine! They are discontented, and their land is stained red from their constant battles. We have done an excellent job."

15

ut Bochica did not see things this way. He was barely able to recognize the people he had created and taught to love one another.

Chibchacum had never forgotten his resentment toward Bochica and wanted to insult him in a way he would never forget. He decided the best way to hurt Bochica was to hurt the people he loved so much.

With an evil incantation, he breathed clouds across the sky, blocking out even the tiniest ray of sunshine.

Then Chibchacum summoned all the sadness of the world and turned it into tears. He poured the tears into the clouds. He pushed his hands down upon the clouds, unleashing a downpour of rain. Only Chie was saved, because Chibchacum kept her close by on an empty cloud.

As the simple homes filled with rainwater, the people raced up the **Andean Mountains** to escape death, and they prayed to Bochica. "We see that we have abandoned you. Please do not abandon us! Chibchacum is a false god! We will follow your teachings once again. Bochica, please give us another chance!"

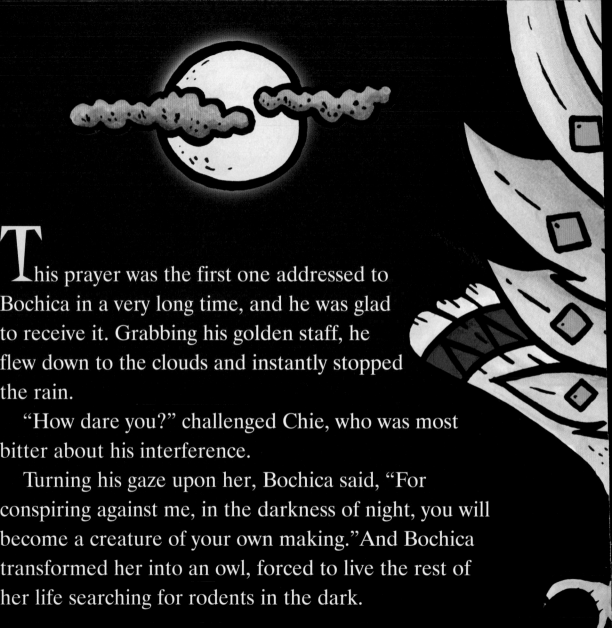

This prayer was the first one addressed to Bochica in a very long time, and he was glad to receive it. Grabbing his golden staff, he flew down to the clouds and instantly stopped the rain.

"How dare you?" challenged Chie, who was most bitter about his interference.

Turning his gaze upon her, Bochica said, "For conspiring against me, in the darkness of night, you will become a creature of your own making." And Bochica transformed her into an owl, forced to live the rest of her life searching for rodents in the dark.

Then Bochica turned his attention to his near-drowning people. With the force of a million thunderbolts, he struck his golden staff into the land, tearing a deep cut into the Earth. This tear ripped and ripped until it tore out of Colombia and reached the **Caribbean Sea**. Immediately, the rainwater flowed into the trench and followed its course to the ocean.

As the water drained away from the land, Bochica transformed his energy into a hot, drying sun. The sun's rays reached down to the Earth, soothing the faces of the desperate people. Soon the people descended from the high **cordilleras** and returned to their villages.

First, the people offered up their gratitude to Bochica. As he bent forward to see his people, the light became a glorious rainbow, stretching over the land.

Once the people were safe, Bochica decided he had to punish Chibchacum.

28

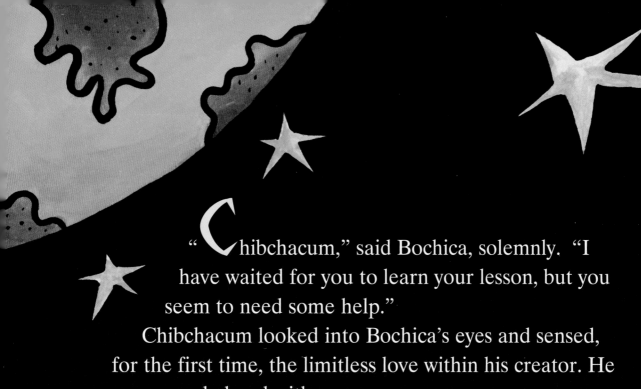

"Chibchacum," said Bochica, solemnly. "I have waited for you to learn your lesson, but you seem to need some help."

Chibchacum looked into Bochica's eyes and sensed, for the first time, the limitless love within his creator. He was overwhelmed with remorse.

"Your lesson," said Bochica, "will be to love the people of the Earth, like a mother loves her baby."

Then, gently, he picked up the Earth and laid it upon Chibchacum's shoulders. Thus, the world was permanently attached to him.

"The **Pachamama** is now a part of you," explained Bochica, "much the way you and the people are a part of me.

Slowly, Chibchacum came to regard the Earth and its people with love and respect. Indeed, he cradled the world with the gentleness of a mother holding her newborn.

The waterways that Bochica cut into the Earth are major rivers, and the surrounding land is very fertile, known for producing fine coffee, bananas, cotton, rice and flowers.

The Chibcha people have never forgotten the kindness of Bochica. And, to this day, it is said that whenever a rainbow appears in Colombia, the people remember the love of their creator.

Glossary

Andean Mountains (andy IN) – a mountain chain in Colombia

bigotry (BIG a tree) – the acts or beliefs of one who is intolerant of other people's views and beliefs

Bochica (bo CHEE cha) – the supreme god of Chibcha mythology who saved humankind from a flood with his golden staff

Caribbean Sea (car IB bee en) - a tropical body of water adjacent to the Atlantic Ocean and southeast of the Gulf of Mexico, and is bounded on the south by Venezuela, Colombia, and Panama

Chibcha (chib CHAH) - also called Muisca, South American Indians who at the time of the Spanish conquest occupied the high valleys surrounding Bogotá and Tunja in Colombia

Chibchacum (chib CHAH cum) – a god in Chibcha mythology, responsible for flooding the earth

Chie (CHEE) – a female in Chibcha mythology, who helped Chibchacum bring a great flood and was punished by Bochica who turned her into an owl

Colombia (col UM bee ah) – a country in Northern South America, bordering the Caribbean Sea, between Panama and Venezuela, and bordering the North Pacific Ocean, between Ecuador and Panama.

cordilleras (cor dee eh rahs) – Spanish for mountain ranges.

Pachamama (pa cha MAH ma) – from the Chibcha language, meaning Mother Earth.

About The Author

Sandy Sepehri lives with her husband, Shahram, and their three children in Florida. She has a bachelor's degree and writes freelance articles and children's stories.